A LETTER

ADDRESSED TO

"J. N. D."

RESPECTING HIS

TRACT ON ETERNAL PUNISHMENT.

BY

JOHN FAWCETT.

"Peace, good will towards men."—Luke, ii. 14.

BRIGHTON.

1848.

A LETTER, &c.

DEAR SIR,

I am favoured by the receipt of a tract, with the initials " J. N. D.," entitled " Brief Scriptural Evidence on the Doctrine of Eternal Punishment, for plain people, with answers to some objections." As I am not informed who has so obligingly forwarded the same, I shall for convenience sake, conclude it was yourself, and address you accordingly.

It is intimated in your first sentence, that the calling in question the truth of the dogma of endless punishment has " shaken the minds of the simple, and has overthrown the faith of some." Your meaning in this sentence is not, to my apprehension, sufficiently explicit. I presume you do not mean to elevate the dogma in dispute to the position of a fundamental doctrine, as a part of the glad tidings to all people? Though not expressly asserted, yet alas! such by inference, and by the conduct of the party with whom you act, I am but too fearful that such is your meaning. You and your party have so treated brethren whose minds have been enlightened, to see the falsehood of this dogma. And it has

B

come to pass at Brighton, and at other places, that if this *"creedy"* ingredient of modern faith is wanting, it is not meet to open the Bible with such believers; or if found unexpectedly at the same prayer meeting, and invited to bless the Lord Christ in a hymn of praise, then is it perfectly consistent immediately to quit the prayer meeting; and as to breaking bread or holding fellowship, is beside the question altogether. So that to all intents and purposes, deficiency of faith in this dogma brands a Christian man as a heretic, or, to use your own expression, he becomes one whose faith has been overthrown. Such is a short outline of the treatment that, during the past year and upwards, I have received from some portions (for there are honourable exceptions) of the so called evangelical parties in this town. And during this period, as my only means of recording testimony, I have put forth several publications under the cognomen of " Paroikos." I have not however been cheered with any notice of these publications until I was favoured by your tract, and I find occasion to rejoice at the intimation your first sentence contains, (my strictures notwithstanding) that " the minds of the simple have been shaken, and faith in this God dishonouring dogma in some happy instances overthrown."

Your animadversions about Greek are very likely to impose on simple and plain (*i. e.,* ignorant) people, and to add in other respects to your worthy reputation, that of being very learned in that language, and a great propounder of the original Scriptures. But, in reply to all your insinuations and open charges, I have simply to ask what profound acquaintance with Greek is necessary rightly to comprehend one or two particular words in that language? Many Greek words, in consequence of use, have now become English words, and this discussion bids fairly to add *aion, hades, gehenna, ktisis, psuche,* and *pneuma,* to our nomenclature. That the word *aion,* and its adjective *aionios,* do not mean eternity, in all passages where they occur, none deny; and to give them such a meaning would often be repugnant to sense and truth. For instance, if *aion* in the following passages was translated *eternity,* what confusion would occur:—"Against the rulers of the darkness of this eternity." Again—"Where is the wise, where is the scribe, where is the disputer of this eternity? The seed among the thorns also would become the cares of this eternity!" In Rom. xii. 2, 1 Tim. vi. 17, Eph. ii. 2, the word denotes past time. In Matt. xii. 32, it denotes future and present. The Septuagint, in Exodus xv. 18, Dan. xii. 3, and Mic. iv. 5, add the words *ete* and *epekeina,* in order to give the idea of prolonged duration to *aion,* which may be rendered thus : "The Lord shall reign through the ages, and further." "The righteous shall shine through the ages, and beyond them;" and, "We will walk in the name of Jehovah our God through the ages, and beyond them." As also in 2 Cor. v. 17, we have another instance in which an intense expression is used to supply the eternal weight of glory; see Greek. This is a remarkable instance of *aionois* failing to express the idea of elongating or unlimited eternity. The lightness of the affliction is contrasted with the eternal weight of glory. *Kath huperboleen eis huperboleen.* Greek scholars declare, says Mr. Forbes, that this expression is infinitely emphatic, and that it is incapable of being expressed in any translation. In fact, that all hyperbole falls short of describing the weight of *aionial* glory; it is so solid, so lasting, that you may pass from one hyperbole to another, and yet when you have gained the last, find yourself infinitely below the idea of that glory. Now if the word *aionial* had this power, why all this infinite emphatic *kath huperboleen eis ¯huperboleen?* Beza tells us it is *æternitas ipsa æternitata majis æternæ*. In Gen. ix. 16, and xvii. 8, 13, we have the *aionial* covenant clearly a limited signification. These words, then, do not undeviatingly mean eternal, but are modified by the subject with which they are connected. The rainbow, circumcision, suffering, and punishment, are words that in themselves only justify our applying a modified construction. On the other hand, Jehovah and his life, are words which of themselves convey an unlimited, unmodified construction; and when we add *aionios,* or eternal to them, we have emphatically the idea of endless existence. It cannot possibly import any other interpretation; while endless punishment is an inconceivable thing, if not a contradiction of terms; or, as the able author above quoted forcibly observes, " means tending to exhaustion, yet constantly operating, and never reaching any defined end."*

But a truce for the present to Greek words— let us come to the consideration of the realities of our religion. What do the Scriptures testify that Christ hath accomplished for this world? They inform us that the Father sent the Son to be

* See his learned and interesting volume on the Nature and Duration of Future Punishments.

the Saviour of the World, *i. e.*, of all, not
of some. 1 John iv. 14; see also John iv. 42;
Luke, iii. 6; Acts, xiii. 47; 1 Tim. iv. 10;
Titus, iii. 4; and, further, "God was in Christ
reconciling the world unto himself," 2 Cor. v. 19.
I believe God's own testimony of his own
glorious, unconditional salvation; and on the
authority of that testimony, the Apostles beseech
all men to be reconciled to God. Those who,
through grace, become the reconciled children of
God, come under the conditions or laws of their
Father's house, though their admission into the
household of faith is solely of grace; for this
there is no law or condition of any description
whatever to be obeyed, for the simple reason of
man's inability to render obedience to any divine
law, as ground of acceptance. It is through grace
and grace alone they believe that in Christ Jesus
they are saved, that in Christ Jesus they have
eternal life, and through this grace they now have
eternal life within them, and will finally issue in
their being with the Lord in his kingdom and
glory. By grace they are now partakers of that,
which ultimately will be found the common and
great salvation for all men.

The statements of the English translation of the
New Testament, you say, are substantially right;
and considering the time and circumstances under
which that translation was made, its general cor-
rectness is acknowledged; but this admission at
once proclaims the fact that many things need cor-
rection, and that plain people, after all, have only
a *substantially* right translation on which to judge
the matter now under discussion. The present
opinion, however, of plain, simple people, regard-

ing their English Testament is, that it is *entirely
right*, and they plead for its plenary verbal in-
spiration. And, taking advantage of this preju-
dice, you dogmatise accordingly; but allow me to
say, that the honest interpretation of Scripture
does not warrant the conclusion you attempt to
palm upon them. It is dishonest—aye, to throw
back upon you your own unqualified expressions,
—" it is flagrantly dishonest, contradictory, and fal-
lacious ;" and, further, I hesitate not to declare, it
subverts every attribute of God, and is alike dishonouring to his holiness and love.

You support your argument by quoting upwards
of fifty texts of Scripture, some of which refer to
the church, others to exclusion from the kingdom,
others to judgments on men in the flesh, but all
made by you to refer to endless punishment, and
are all classed together and made unitedly to testify to what they do not testify, and are conse-
quently by you wrested to an unholy purpose.
Those in which the Greek words *hades* (the grave)
and *gehenna* (the judgment by fire in the Valley of
the Son of Hinnom) occur, are allowed to stand
translated by the English word HELL, (Saxon, a
hole,) which term the plain and simple people for
whom you write, associate with all the frightful
popular notions attached to that word. For the
benefit of those likely to be deluded by your name
and influence, I insert an explanation of these
words.*

Αἰών, Age.

From 'αεὶ, ever, and ὢν, being; aiōn or æon, age, era, or
period of indefinite duration.

The ages,—*the worlds*, Heb. i. 2, xi. 3; this age,—*this world*,
Mat. xiii. 22, Mark iv. 19, Luke xvi. 8, xx. 34, (*that world*) 35,

After your array of misapplied quotations, you proceed to inform plain people that " men" (by which appellation I suppose you refer to Chris-

Rom. xii. 2, 1 Cor. i. 20, ii. 6, 8, iii. 18, 2 Cor. iv. 4, Gal. i. 4, Eph. vi. 12; the present age,—*this world* or *this present world*, Mat. xii. 32, Eph. i. 21, 1 Tim. vi. 17, 2 Tim. iv, 10, Tit. ii. 12; the age of this world,—*the course of this world*, Eph. ii. 2; the completion of the age,—*the end of the world*, Mat. xiii. 39, 40, 49, xxxiv. 3, xxviii. 20, (ages) Heb. xi. 26; the ends of the ages,—*the ends of the world*, 1 Cor. x. 11; the coming age,—*the world to come*, Mark x. 30, Luke xviii. 30, Heb. vi. 5; the coming ages,—*the ages to come*, Eph. ii. 7; before the ages, *before the world*, 1 Cor. ii. 7; from the age or ages,—*since the world began or beginning of the world*, Luke i. 70, John ix. 32, Acts iii. 21, xv. 18, Eph. iii. 9, *from ages*, Col. i. 26; in the age,—*while the world standeth*, 1 Cor. viii. 13; unto all the generations of the age of the ages,—*throughout all ages, world without end*, Eph. iii. 21.

Other words also occur in the original, translated *world*, where they do not refer to time; namely, kosmos and oikoumenos.

The purpose of the ages,—*the eternal purpose*, Eph. iii. 11; the King of the ages,—*the King eternal*, 1 Tim. i. 17.

Not— in the age,—*never*, Mark iii. 29, John iv. 14, viii. 51, 52, xi. 26, xiii. 8.

In or unto (that is, during) the age or ages; the age of the age, or the ages of the ages; the ages; all the ages (Jude 25); the day of the age, (2 Pet. iii. 18); *ever, for ever, for ever and ever, for evermore*, in 53 passages in the New Testament, which may be readily found by a common Concordance.

Αἰώνιος, aiōnian or age during.

Adjective derived from aiōn; æonion, connected with an age.

Aiōnian or age during,—*for ever*, Philemon 15.

Before the aiōnian or age during times (that is, the times of the ages); *before the world began*, 2 Tim. i. 9, Tit. i. 2.

From aiōnian times,—*since the world began*, Rom. xvi. 25.

Aiōnian or age during,—*eternal or everlasting*; fire, punishment, damnation, judgment, destruction, salvation, redemption, consolation, covenant, inheritance, habitations, house, things, power, glory and weight of glory, gospel, Kingdom, Spirit, God, in 22 passages in the New Testament; and life, in 44.

In Rom. i. 20 *(eternal power)* and Jude 6 *(everlasting chains)* the Greek word is αἴδιος, also derived from 'αεί, always for ever.

In the Old Testament the terms *ever, for ever, everlasting* in the English version, correspond with the same Greek words in the Septuagint. Thus Canaan is promised for an aiōnian possession to Abraham, Gen. xvii. 8, to Jacob, xlviii. 4, to the Jews,

tians who differ from you) " seek to evade these plain testimonies, and begin to reason, and speak Greek." It would have been well, sir, if you had

from age unto age, Jer. xxv. 5; the throne to David's son, during the age, 1 Chr. xvii. 14; the priesthood to Aaron and his sons, unto (or during) the age, Exod. xl. 15, to Phinehas and his sons, aiōnian or age during, Num. xxv. 13; all these referring, primarily at least, to the earthly Canaan and to Israelites after the flesh. In Gen. xlix. 26, we read of the aénnaōn or overflowing hills; in Hab. iii. 6, of the aiōnian hills; his ways aiōnian; in Isaiah lvii. 15, of the high and lofty one who inhabiteth the age.

Can any other conclusion be drawn from these plain statements but that the terms themselves imply only *indefinite* duration, and that the particular nature or extent of that duration must be determined by the nature of the subject with which they are connected?

"Αδης, Hades.

From *a*, negative, and εἰδω, to see; the unseen, invisible, or hidden place; the state of the dead.

Translated *Hell* in Mat. xi. 23, xvi. 18, Luke x. 15, xvi. 23, Acts ii. 27, 31, Rev. i. 18, vi. 18, xx. 13, 14; *Grave* in 1 Cor. xv. 55.

In the Old Testament, Hades in the Septuagint corresponds to *Hell* in the English version, (except in 2 Sam. xxii. 6, Prov. v. 5, death, and Ezek. xxxii. 21, pit,) as in Job xxvi. 6, Psl. ix. 17, xvi. 10, cxvi. 3, Jonah ii. 2;—27 times. It also frequently corresponds to *the Grave,* as in Gen. xxxvii. 35, Job xiv. 13, Psl. lxxxviii. 3, Hosea xiii. 14. Let the reader substitute *Hell* for the grave in these passages; if a believer in eternal torments, could he then join in Job's prayer? (as in xiv. 13.)

Γεέννα, Gehenna.

From the Hebrew;—the valley of Hinnom, where all the filth of Jerusalem was thrown, and consumed by fires kept constantly burning there.

Translated *Hell* in Mat. v. 22, 29, 30, x. 28, xviii. 9, xxiii. 15, 33, Mark ix. 43, 45, 47, Luke xii. 5, James iii. 6.

The term does not occur in the Old Testament in the Septuagint, but the valley or sepulchre of Hinnom or the son of Hinnom is referred to in Josh. xv. 8, 2 Kings xxiii. 10, 2 Chr. xxviii. 3, xxxiii. 6, Jer. xix. 2, 6, xxxii. 35. In Jerem. xix. 6, the prophet predicts that it shall be called " the valley of slaughter," the emblem of destruction.—*Vide an interesting publication by* DAVID WALDIE, *entitled " The Ultimate Manifestation of God to the World;" published by H. K. Lewis, 15, Gower Street, North.*

condescended rightly to have informed yourself of
their reasons, and submitted your own, as well as
to have met their Greek with Greek. But instead
of such sturdy honesty, you content yourself with
the weapons of defamation, and have the temerity
to call their reasons evasions, their use of Greek
dishonest. Truth pities and smiles at your imbe-
cility. You evidently have not made yourself
acquainted with what, under the name of univer-
salism, you have dared to assail. O sir! Christ is
a King, and also a Creator. He has a kingdom
and also a world to make new. This kingdom
and this world are conducted by him, who through
the blood of the *æonian* covenant, has become the
God and Father of these coming *aions*. The *pro-*
totokos, the first begotten of every creature, Col.
i. 5; the first begotten from the dead, Rev. i. 5;
the very image or similitude of God, the great
revealer of God; all the works of Jesus showing
forth God, even from the invisible greatness discovered by the telescope, to the invisible minuteness discovered by the microscope, all things, great
and small, utter forth his wisdom, power, and
goodness; while manifested in flesh, and in resurrection, man is declared the object of his tender
solicitude and love. The being on whom God
has lavished all the wonders of his power in
creation, is yet destined, though now, in an evil
and fallen condition, to shew forth the resplendent
splendour and image of his great and glorious
Head, in resurrection, in incorruption, in glory,
in power, and in a spiritual body. As it is written,
"The first Adam was made a living soul, or creature, the last Adam a quickening spirit." And as
all have borne the image of the earthy, all shall also

bear the image of the heavenly. Oh, dear sir, if you knew the truth, you could never have so scandalised it as to speak of it as you do in your two following flippant systems :—

"Now there are two systems, by which men seek to set aside these plain passages. One is that all will be saved, all, even the Devil himself, though some few of them do not like to say anything so plain as that. The other is, that the wicked will not be saved, but that the soul is not immortal at all, and that the fire of hell will in time consume them."

I almost wish there was such a fire as is here alluded to, that all the errors of modern theology might be committed to its flames, and then Christians would not be so distracted by what man's wisdom teacheth, as to love what the Holy Spirit teacheth. If, sir, it is God's prerogative to bring good out of evil, light out of darkness, beauty out of deformity, harmony out of discord, paradise out of chaos, and resurrection out of corruption ; who shall dare to limit the Divine Being, and say he is not able and willing to bring happiness out of misery, and *aonian* life and gain out of *aonian* loss and death ? " There shall be " (says God, not man, or any set of men) " no more death, neither sorrow, nor crying, neither shall there be any more pain ; for the former things are passed away ; and he that sat upon the throne, said, Behold ! I make all things new !" Again : " Every creature which is in heaven, and on earth, and under the earth, and such as are in the sea, and all that are in them, heard I saying, Blessing, and honour, and glory, and power, be unto him that sits upon the throne, and unto the Lamb to the *æons* of the *æons*. The last enemy that shall be invalidated is death. O death, I will be thy dissolution or perdition, not plagues. And

Jehovah shall take away—the veil that is spread over all nations, and will awaken up death in triumphant perpetuity of life; and God will wipe away tears from all faces, and the disgrace of his people shall he take away from all the earth." So saith the Lord, and I for one rejoice to testify that I believe the word of the Lord, and that verily there shall be a fulfilment of these things which the Lord hath spoken, " for good is the word of the Lord."

The Scripture no where says the human soul is in its own nature immortal,* but, on the contrary, it testifies that God only hath immortality, and that it is produced in us out of an incorruptible seed by the logos of the living God, who abideth

* Mr. J. N. Darby, in his tract, "The Hopes of the Church," thus gives his testimony on this subject. "The idea (says he) of a resurrection of the just was familiar to the disciples of Christ, and such is represented as to happen in Luke, xiv. 14. 'Thou shalt be recompensed at the resurrection of the just.' But before coming to direct proofs we would express our convictions, that the idea of the immortality of the soul has no source in the gospel; that it comes, on the contrary, from the Platonist's, and that it was just when the coming of Christ was denied in the Church, or at least began to be lost sight of, that the doctrine of the immortality of the soul came in to replace that of the resurrection. This was about the time of Origen. It is hardly needful to say that we do not doubt the immortality of the soul; we only assert that this view has taken the place of the doctrine of the resurrection of the Church, as the epoch of its joy and glory." In a note he adds, " As to that expression, 2 Tim. i, 10, ' brought life and immortality to light;' immortality signifies the incorruptibility of the body, and not the immortality of the soul."

Those who desire instruction on this interesting and important subject, will find themselves fully repaid by the perusal of a series of tracts published by " Abiezer," being three letters in vindication of the whole counsel of God, addressed to the Plymouth Brethren, and against some objections of a Baptist minister. These learned and able productions of " Abiezer's" are unanswered, and unanswerable.—J. F.

continually. You, sir, on the contrary, assert that it is immortal; and you support your contradictions of the word of God by the question, "How come the wicked to be alive after death in order to be punished? Where do they get this life?" Sir, your question will eat as doth a canker, for your reply that "they cannot be alive to be punished at all," overthrows faith in the resurrection. Acts xxvi. 8. Man's immortality is bound up in his resurrection, and two periods of resurrection are clearly and explicitly revealed, one of the just, the other of the unjust. Honour and privilege to the first, judgment to the second. The day of the Lord's judgment is now misjudged by man as a time for consigning the myriads left out of the election of eternal life, to endless torments; while God blessedly tells us, it will be "the times of the restitution of all things."

Your elegant parallel between Adam's immortality and a child being whipped, if it is worth any thing, goes to illustrate the truth for which I contend. The child being in a whippable condition, was liable to be so dealt with; man being in a mortal condition, was liable to its consequences. If it had been both physically and morally impossible to have whipped the child, the child never could have been whipped; if it had been both physically and morally impossible for Adam to have died, he could not have been thus punished. He would then, in his own fleshly nature, which was of the earth, have been immortal, and *death* could not have entered through his criminality.

Again, you say death is not ceasing to exist, because after that comes the judgment. True, but the judgment is in resurrection life. "All that are in their graves shall hear his voice, and shall come forth; they that have done good, unto the resurrection of life; they that have done evil, to the resurrection of judgment." Life is again given, so it must have ceased during the dominion of death, or death would cease to be death. But your system, among its many crudities, involves the idea that death is life. The body dead, the immortal soul of man alive! Scripture no where so represents the state of the wicked. I challenge you to produce an instance in which the Scriptures so speak of man. But on this subject you have favoured plain people with an attempt at arguing the point.

" But were it even not thus disproved by the Apostles' statement, there is another thing remains : if Adam's sin brought in death on all his posterity, and man is not immortal, for that is their doctrine, where do sinners get the life from after death, that is, after ceasing to exist at all? Their sins cannot give it them. They tell us that death having been pronounced on man, there is no immortality, no life but in Christ. Well then, see what it comes to, the wicked have life in Christ in order to be punished for their sins, and this life which they have in Christ is not eternal life, for if it be, they must be (if not eternally happy or saved) eternally miserable. And moreover, this life which they have of Christ to be punished in, is to be consumed by the wrath and punishment of God. If it is not life in and from Christ, then death does not put an end to a man; death is not what they pretend it is, man is, in a word, an immortal being. And further, what was the worth of Christ's death? Some of them say it was just simply death as the wages of sin. But he bore our sins, and if so, our sins being merely a measured quantity of punishment, it is not the wrath of God due to us as lost sinners, but merely a partial punishment he had to avert. But further, as regards the wicked: the death of Christ they say averted death from them so that they should be punished. He did not bear their sins, that is clear, for it is for them they are to be punished; so that Christ's death was necessary to keep alive the wicked in order to punish, and then consume them, and was applied to this purpose by God."

You must excuse my telling you, sir, that the above passage is, in my plain judgment, a mixture of mysticism and misapprehension. It imputes, asserts, and attempts deductions from uncertain and assumed premises, after a fashion that every well instructed Christian must deplore. By way of reply, I would take leave to recapitulate in other words what I have advanced above, that in Christ alone is life, *zoe;* all life is derived from Christ. "In him was life, and the life was the light of men." The life having caught hold of dying man, nailed that dying nature to the cross, placed it in the grave, and from thence brought up life in resurrection, blessedness, and incorruption. The immortality of man, therefore, rests upon this rock, the incarnation, death, burial, and resurrection of Jesus. All men are interested in what the Redeemer of the world has accomplished in his great salvation. Though some, through grace, believe these things, and some do not believe, their unbelief cannot make void the fact of God's truth. Believers have peculiar privileges and duties; they are now united to Christ, they are one with him; and though in consequence of their union with Adam, they die, they now have the title and earnest to eternal life in resurrection; while those who do not believe, are unreconciled, know nothing of union or spirituality, and have in them no principle of eternal life; they are dead while they live, yet they are to live in resurrection; and though they rise to judgment, and to receive the due reward of their deeds, yet scripture does not represent punishment as the end for which they rise, but restoration. Punishment may be one of the means employed by God to that glorious end; but I go not beyond the record—Scripture is silent as to the means; while

Col. i. 20, and similar passages, afford ground for the happiest confidence as to the end; and as to the means, we may well exclaim with the patriarch, "Shall not the Judge of all the earth do what is right?" One thing is clearly revealed, that when the unbeliever is raised, he will eventually find that the blessed fact he was called on to believe while in his flesh and blood state, is still a glorious truth, and that Christ is still his Saviour, and that he will be saved. Your system involves the monstrous idea that Jesus will be the destroyer, not the Saviour of the creatures he has redeemed; that the great Redeemer is not the express image of the unchangeable God without shadow of turning, but that he who you now represent as Saviour, and call upon the wicked to turn from their wickedness and live, to him who has redeemed them, will after all be found never to have redeemed them, never to have been their Saviour, but from all eternity to have planned their subjection to vanity here, and damnation hereafter, and that damnation to be eternal life in misery. Eternal God! what thoughts are thy children holding of thee? Oh, send forth the light of thy holy truth into their hearts, that they may be delivered from such error and evil.

I beg to observe on your concluding remarks, that the expressions, "Their end is destruction, —They shall not see life—They have never forgiveness—They have no life in them—Christ will deny them—He never knew them"—have no reference whatever to the subject.

The point at issue is simply this,—is the punishment of the wicked endless? is there no restoration promised in sacred scripture to them? You know, or ought to know, that all those expressions have reference solely to the exclusion from the kingdom of Christ. That at the revelation of that kingdom, none but partakers of the first resurrection enter, is fully and freely admitted as the clear testimony of scripture; but your assumption, that exclusion from the kingdom necessarily establishes your frightful dogma, is as gratuitous as it is unscriptural. To the holding this error may be traced the present Pharisaical state of professing Christians. To illustrate what I mean, I will tell you of a little intercourse I had the other day with two brethren. I will copy it exactly from my memorandum book, as I wrote it down the day after it occurred:

I was walking up the Western Road on Saturday, 25th September, 1847, when I met Lord Congleton and Mr. Hargrove, and the following conversation took place. After usual salutations and enquiries for mutual friends, H. commenced—

H.—Well, you could not answer my objections to your views in the case of Judas. Good for that man if he had never been born; and yet according to your opinion, an eternity of happiness awaited him.

F.—Yes, I consider that I demolished your argument in the Berean Letters, page 21.

H.—No; that mode of accommodation of scripture will not do.

F.—You have no authority for accommodating that scripture, which of itself is silent on the point, for promulgating the endless nature of punishment.

H.—Do you believe that the sins of mankind committed against the knowledge of the Gospel, are venial?

F.—Yes, I do.

H.—You hold that there will be eventual universal pardon for every sin ever committed, whatever its nature or degree?

F.—Yes, I believe that God will ultimately pardon the whole of mankind.

C. repeated John iii. 36.

F.—If you quote that passage in such connection, you assert your belief in annihilation, and deny the resurrection of the unjust. They shall not see life.

C. (startled)—No, by no means.

F.—Well, then they are to see life. It will not do to found or oppose any doctrine on an isolated passage. 1 John v. 12, is the best explanation of John iii. 36.

H.—Scripture, I admit, is full of passages on your side of the question. I have no objection to a Christian holding these views, provided he keeps them to himself; but I must say I was grieved when I heard the position you had assumed here, and that you were publicly propounding these views.

F.—They are either true, or they are erroneous. If true, as I firmly believe them to be, I have no option left but to propound them.

H.—Yes, but the question is, are they true? and there not being so, but error, you ought not to propound them. Besides, the choicest of God's saints are so grieved and so opposed to your proceedings.

F.—I have nothing to do with what the saints say or think, unless their words and thoughts are in accordance with Scripture. I appeal to Scripture.

H.—Yes, you are right there; they must bring all to Scripture.

F.—Well, what saith one of its most solemn texts? " If I be lifted up, I will draw all unto me."

H.—Yes, but there is John iii. 36.

F.—Yes, but there is John i. 29.

H.—Well, dear brother, the Lord deliver you. I do not suppose, if we stood here for the next 24 hours, we should convince you.

F.—Certainly not. But what has the Lord to deliver me out of?

H.—Error.

F.—If in error, pray shew me in what it consists.

C.—I could not sit down to the Bible with any person who so constructed and explained Scripture.

F.—That is Pharisaism. The principles you defend are those which have brought the church into its present Pharisaical state.

C.—Farewell.

H.—Farewell.

F.—Farewell.

Now, dear sir, to your tract again. You challenge any man who knows Greek, to produce one passage where the word *æonian* refers to the millennium kingdom. No well instructed universalist ever called the millennium age the whole of Christ's reign; though mere millenarians must necessarily make this mistake, because they put a part for the whole. Millennium not being a scriptural term at all, and only used conventionally to express the age referred to in Rev. xx. 6. It is a Latin expression, used instead of an English one to translate the Greek word *kilion,* a thousand.

This being the commencement of the *æreas* or *aions*, when the Lord Jesus shall take unto himself his great power and reign (see 1 Tim. i. 17,) where "king eternal" is in the Greek, king of the ages or *aions*, of which period popularly called the millennium is the first *aion*; but Christ will reign through and beyond the *aions*, for he must reign till he has subdued all his enemies, and he cannot fully stand in the place of the second Adam until all creation is delivered from all the evil brought upon it by the first Adam, when having finished his service to God and man in this wise, all things, the Father excepted, shall be put under him; and the enemy and the avenger being stilled, his name which is above every name, shall be excellent in all the earth. Of the subsequent dealings of God with man throughout eternity, (which has been happily stated by the poor deaf and dumb boy to mean "the life time of the Almighty,") we at present know nothing; neither indeed many things which are to occur intermediately; but this we do know, that we are in a Father's and a Saviour's hands, who in the midst of judgment remembers mercy, and for whose *pleasure* we are and were created. I answer your challenge, therefore, by observing how unenlightened and uninformed the challenger must be, for no enlightened or instructed believer ever said the millennium was the *aionial* kingdom.

You favour us with a word of Greek in your last page. You say—"The etymology given as early as the time of Aristotle, and by him, is *aien on*—always existing,—and that the earliest use of the word is in the sense of a man's life." Well and good; the word is derived from the verb *a o*—to breathe, (Latin, *spiro)*, and is compounded of the Alpha and Omega of the Greek alphabet, signifying that the continuity of man's life from first to last is in the action of the breath of his nostrils. Therefore, a man, while he is alive, lives uninterruptedly, and not by fits and starts, till death comes; and *anephneusen aiona*, just means breathing time; on which ground I can well afford to congratulate you upon your heathen authorities.— Compare Gen. ii. 7, and James iv. 14. But before I dismiss the Greek, I would take occasion to say that the Grecians had three words in use to denote time in its several gradations, *kairos, chronos,* and *aion.* By *aion,* they meant an age, by *chronos,* a time of considerable continuance, and by *kairos,* a short inconsiderable time. So that *kairos* and *aion* are two extremes of *time,* having *chronos* for their medium; and by this means, *kairos* and *aion* oppose each other in a very natural antitheses.

While the Jews, with the Scriptures in their hands, supposed that the whole counsel of God was included in their two *aions* of the Mosaic dispensation, or age that then existed; and the age to come, when the kingdom was again to be restored to Israel under their Messiah; they entirely overlooked the fact that the Gentiles were to be fellow-heirs in the kingdom. (Eph. iii. 1—13, Acts xv. 17.) Their prophets had testified of this, —(Rom. xvi. 25, 26; Eph. i. 9, 10; 1 Peter i. 10—12),—as well as their future ingathering, the rise of anti-Christ, and the consummation, when the stone was to fall upon the image, but they saw it not; so, without noticing Gentile mistakes and misapprehensions, we at once declare how light we hold the assistance afforded by Aristotle, Greeks, and Jews, and turn to the Scriptures as our only authority. In them we are clearly informed of at least seven *aions*, which, to illustrate my meaning, I may as well submit, as conveying an outline of their order and character :—

1. Adamic.
2. Noahtic, or Patriarchal.
3. Mosaic, or Israel.
4. The Election of Jew and Gentile to the Kingdom.
5. The First Resurrection and Millennium.
6. The Second Resurrection and Subjection of all to Christ.
7. God all in all. (1 Cor. xi. 28.)

And, dear sir, do you now ask me how many *aions* there are beyond these seven? May I not well reply in the words of the Saviour?—"I say not unto thee seven, but seventy times seven;" and that will not exhaust the display of the infinite glory of our Father, who is love, in blessing those who by nature were his enemies. "I say unto you, love your enemies; bless them."

In bidding you farewell, dear sir, allow me to say that any strong expression contained in this letter is dictated by a sense of the importance of that which in faithfulness and in confidence I believe to be God's truth, and in sincere good-will to you, and all who so differ from me. Those brethren who see with me, do not judge God as you assert; but those who see with you, assume the office of the judgment seat. It is you who decide, and that too on the interpretation of a disputed Greek word, what the judgment on the unjust shall be both as to condition and duration, *i. e.*, endless torment. Ponder this conclusion. To my mind it is so awful and so erroneous, that, through grace, I am determined, as long as I have a hand to write and a tongue to proclaim God's love, (which, to support your endless torment system, you dare to write "He is love; but he is God, and acts freely and holily in his love. God is love, but it is God that is so. Love is what he is." Attempting to separate love from God in some of his actions and judgments) to be found ever testifying that God is love in all and to all; and enlightened by his spirit, perceive with all joy that his holy anger and his consuming fire, are but emanations of love, that will burn up what is noxious to true life, and consume that only which ought to die.

In conclusion, you say, " as has been remarked by others, that if God meant to convey the idea of eternal punishment, he would not have used expressions stronger than he has used, nor do any exist." The reply is simply the truth, that *aionial* punishment is not endless misery; and men, by their misuse of a Greek word, and their ignorance of the plan of redemption in and by Christ Jesus, have imputed this frightful, wretched idea, to the holy and blessed judgments of the Lord. Yet, dear sir, mistake me not; it remains a most important enquiry, who shall and who shall not enjoy the glory which is to be displayed when Jesus comes in his kingdom, 1 Cor. vi. 9, 11. Let such, hearing that there is mercy with the Lord, that he may be feared, now flee from the wrath to come, and be found washed and sanctified by the Spirit of the Redeemer; or there remains a fearful looking for of judgment, and a longsome night of death before the morning shall reveal to them the lingering day of their visitation drawing near. Therefore said the apostle, " Repent, therefore, and turn ye to the blotting out of your sins, when the season of revival shall come from the presence of the Lord; and when he shall send forth Jesus Christ, who hath been before manifested to you; whom heaven must receive until the times of the restitution of all things, of which God hath always spoken by the mouth of all his holy prophets."

I remain,

Yours very cordially,

J. F.

———

P. S.—DEAR SIR,—After the above letter was in the printer's hands, I received " Philomath's" " comments" on your tract. As his able and masterly production does not interfere with the ground on which this letter is written, I have not considered it necessary or advisable to retire from the field, but rather to take courage, by finding myself beside such a champion. " The testimony of two men is true." And happy shall I be if those who honour this letter with a perusal, will honour " Philomath" likewise. And as " Philomath" and "Paroikos" have both dropped their cognomen, it is hoped that Messrs. Seabrook and Fawcett may receive from you, dear sir, that attention and consideration which probably as anonymous writers they could not expect. Above all, may the blessed truths we have proclaimed (and so glorious are they, that before them we must both feel how imperfect and what injustice our best advocacy has rendered) sound long and sure upon the attention of believers in Christ, that this is the sure Gospel of the great salvation of the Saviour of the world. In him, dear sir, (our differences notwithstanding,) we are dear to one another, and know little of the Unity of the Spirit, if honest differences and hard fought combats for the faith are allowed to dissolve that bond.

Yours truly,

J. F.

J. F. EYLES, PRINTER, 28, WESTERN ROAD, BRIGHTON.

[As my printer informs me I have a blank sheet, I take advantage of it to give the following extract from the life of the late Joseph Blanco White. While it places the subject of endless torment in the extreme light, as held by Roman Catholics, and though its lurid gloom may be somewhat softened by Protestants, yet, in so far as held by either, I take occasion to testify that the dogma is from beneath, from the Father of lies, and not from above, from the Father of love and grace.]

"The third day of the Exercises was known to be the most terrific. The subject appointed for that day was the eternity of punishment. I cannot give an idea of the ingenuity employed in striking the imagination by means of this awful subject. Whatever can be conceived to torture the body and agonize the soul, all was described in the most vivid colours. In the morning, the reading and meditation turned upon the consignment of a wicked soul to hell. The howlings of the evil spirits, as they celebrated their triumph; the first plunging of the wretched being into the flames; its cries of despair, its blasphemies against heaven; the applause with which the most horrible expressions were received by the devil and his angels—all were given with shocking minuteness. The *ejaculations* of the Director added touches of lurid light to the picture; and yet he could not conclude by imploring mercy. That word could not pass his lips. His voice gradually sunk, while sighs and sobs grew louder and louder around him. Perceiving the moment when terror was at the highest, he suddenly assumed a composed and almost familiar tone, assuring his hearers that under the present impressions of his mind, oppressed and sinking as it was under the idea of sin and its appropriate punishment, it was impossible for him to speak of hope, of mercy, of forgiveness. He must, therefore, dismiss his hearers abruptly, and leave them to their own thoughts. He then clapped his hands (the usual signal for departure), and retired into the vestry. As the congregation crossed the small quadrangle before the chapel, on their way to their rooms, you might think you saw forty or fifty prisoners who had received sentence of death a few moments before. Some held their hands before their eyes, and scarcely could keep themselves from crying aloud. Others looked down on the ground in the attitude of utter despair. All seemed absorbed in grief."

www.ingramcontent.com/pod-product-compliance
Lightning Source LLC
Chambersburg PA
CBHW081309040426
42452CB00014B/2710

*9 781535 806572 *